Get That Mouse Out Now!

Written by Elizabeth Sengel

Illustrated by Jackie Urbanovic

STECK-VAUGHN COMPANY

A Division of Harcourt Brace & Company

One day Crowley Mouse decided to go to town. He put on his cap and stepped out of his house. He took the trail that wound down the hill.

Crowley looked around. There were pretty flowers all over the ground. Fluffy white clouds sailed in the sky. The sound of bees filled the air. "How pretty it is outside today!" he said.

Brownie Cow saw Crowley walking along.
"Where are you going?" Brownie called.

"I'm going to town!" Crowley said. He sounded very proud of himself.

Brownie blinked her big round eyes. "Have fun!" she said.

Crowley was hungry when he got to town. He found a place to eat. But when he sat down, a lady shouted. "Eek! It's a mouse!" she yelled.

Everyone ran out.

The cook came out of the kitchen. "What is going on here?" he growled. Then he saw Crowley.

"Get that mouse out now!" he shouted as he pounded on a table.

Crowley ran outside. "Wow!" he said.
"What was all that about?"

8

Crowley stuck a blade of grass in his mouth. "Now what can I do?" he asked. "I know! I'll go shopping! I need some new towels."

Crowley found a bath store downtown. But when he went in, the clerk screamed. "Eek! It's a mouse!" she cried.

Everyone started to run out.

The boss scowled. "Get that mouse out now!" she shouted.

Crowley ran out of the store like a flash.
He wasn't sure whether to run north or south!

Crowley sat down on the ground. "What will I do now?" he said with a frown. "Well, Mom always told me not to pout. Oh, how pretty those flowers are! I want some."

When the flower lady saw Crowley, she shouted. "Eek! It's a mouse!" she yelled.

Flowers and pots flew all about. Someone in the crowd shouted, "Get that mouse out now!"

Crowley ran until he was out of breath. He stopped in front of a toy shop. Then he heard a loud POP! "Eek!" Crowley shouted. "I'm getting out now!"